CU00823140

Contents

Introduction

The Cavapoo is a mixed breed that combines a Poodle's intelligence with the loving nature of a Cavalier King Charles Spaniel. While mixing an aristocratic English breed with a French duck-hunting waterdog might seem odd, the Cavapoo turned out to be the perfect family companion.

This is a small breed with a big heart. Their low shedding coat also makes them perfect for people with allergies. The Cavapoo is a mix of the Poodle (Miniature or Toy) and the Cavalier King Charles Spaniel.

They are easy to care for, very gentle and make wonderful down to earth companions that love to chill on the couch just as much as they love playing in the park. Both of their parent breeds have long histories. The Cavalier King Charles Spaniel was a coveted companion and the Poodle was a hardworking hunting dog.

Mixing these two breeds together creates a very intelligent family companion dog. Also because of their low-allergen coat, the Poodle in this breed makes the Cavapoo great for allergy sufferers. When it comes to looks, they are just like a living teddy bear! They have dark eyes, a button nose and a curly coat. You can expect this mix to be loving and intelligent. They are easy to train and have just the right amount of playful energy for most owners.

The silkiest and smartest pooch on the block, the Cavapoo wins over pet owners with his combination of good looks and a lovely temperament. This mixed breed dog makes an excellent companion and a family pet, so it's no wonder that these guys rank as one of the most popular designer dog breeds. As a hybrid, Cavapoo comes from two purebred parents- the Poodle (miniature or toy) and the Cavalier Kings Charles Spaniel. Cavapoos represent everything designer dogs are about: the best of both parents in one adorable pooch. If you've been considering diving into the exciting world of designers dogs, there's no better place to start that with this little beauty.

There are so many reasons why this incredible pup has become so beloved. The low-shedding Cavapoo is a great companion dog whose small stature makes him a perfect fit for apartment dwellers, seniors, and singles who like to include their pooch in all things social. A gentle nature means this indoor dog is a terrific family pet that does well with older kids who can be taught to appreciate his smaller size.

Read further for more information about cavapoos; how to care for and grom them and also tips on buying them.

What Is A Cavapoo?

When you combine the gentle Miniature Poodle, with the loyal Cavalier King Charles Spaniel, then you get the affectionate dog known as the Cavoodle.These sweet doggies are easily considered one of the most popular designers breeds today and have been increasingly gaining fame for their family-oriented temperament.

Since they are not considered a "purebred" or "pedigree" dog, they are not recognized by the American Kennel Club (AKC). However, as of 2009, they have been approved by the International Designer Canine Registry

Pros:

- A great family companion.
- Perfect amount of playful energy.
- Easy to care for.
- Highly trainable and eager to please.
- Low-allergen coat.

Cons:

- Can be prone to separation anxiety.
- Bark a lot when not trained correctly.
- Grooming can be challenging.
- A very expensive breed.

A Day In The Life Of This Breed

Depending on how you start the day, your Cavapoo will start it at the same pace. Whether you decide to spend a sleepy morning cuddling them, or immediately get ready for the day, your pooch will be by your side ready to continue the day's journey with you.

After a quick walk around the block and a much-needed potty break you can expect them to be relaxed.

If you happen to be a homebody or work at home, your Cavapoo will be at your feet, gnawing on their favorite toy or watching the world go by. However if you need to leave for a while this breed is easy to crate train – they are content spending time in a safe space waiting for you to return as they amuse themselves with a toy.

When you take them out to the park at lunchtime expect to get plenty of attention. This pup will love meeting new people and will be happy receiving strokes from a passerby or sniffing a fellow canine.

At the park they will love any game you give them. Whether you let them play with the other pups at the dog park or spend time tossing a frisbee or a tennis ball, they will be happy. However you do not need to play for long – a good 30 minutes is enough for this breed.

Once they return home they will have a drink of water and will likely be mellowed out for the day. They will be happy for an occasional stroll in the evening should you need an excuse to go outside and enjoy the great outdoors.

Just remember that no matter how you spend your day, they just love spending time by your side. As the day slowly winds down your Cavapoo is likely just as exhausted as you are and is ready to hit the hay. They will either sleep in a crate or snuggled up in bed with you, waiting for another exciting day by your side.

Temperament And Behavior

The Cavapoo has a gentle and loving temperament. They enjoy being around people and are content to spend the day watching the world fly by with you. Because this breed is a mix you cannot guarantee their temperament however you hope they inherit the Poodle's intelligence and Cavalier King Charles Spaniel's kindness.

The Cavapoo has a friendly, loyal and affectionate personality. They're good-natured dogs that are quite sociable with people, dogs, and other pets. Their friendly personality does not deter them from being good watchdogs in the home. They'll bark when strangers come to the home or if they hear strange noises.

They do best when they're around people and not left home alone for long stretches. Cavapoos are not happy when they're being ignored and often suffer from separation anxiety when left alone. This separation anxiety may result in the Cavapoo whining, barking, howling or chewing on things around the home. Fear not...with some good socialization, training, and proper exercise, these habits can be greatly reduced or even eliminated.

This hybrid is playful but not to the point of being overly energetic. Cavapoos enjoy playing fetch or tug of war but they only initiate play when they are bored or have not been exercised. Again because this is a mix each one is different. Some are relaxed like their Cavalier King Charles Spaniel parent while others are a bit more athletic like their Poodle parent.

Their loving nature can be a double-edged sword. As they are incredibly attached to people they are prone to developing separation anxiety. This means when left alone they can be vocal or destructive in a variety of creative ways. The good news is with the correct positive training this can be fixed.

Overall this is a loving hybrid that should get the best attributes from both parents. Just remember that while anxiety is an issue with this breed it is easily fixed with positive reinforcement – remain patient and consistent with your training and socialization.

Cavapoo Dog Appearance

Because this is a mixed breed it is hard to say exactly what your pup will look like. Some look more like their Cavalier King Charles Spaniel parent with longer ears and a loosely curled coat. Whereas others look more like their Poodle parent with a tightly curled coat. However there is no doubt that these dogs look like living teddy bears and are just as cuddly.

Thanks to their Poodle parent, their coat is low shed and leaves less allergy-inducing dander lying around. Their fur grows continuously and is soft to the touch. While there are a variety of haircuts the most common are the Teddy Bear Clip and the Puppy Cut. These two haircuts make the coat shorter and easier to brush – this means less day to day grooming.

Physical Traits

Cavapoos come in one of three coat types: hair, fleece or wool, although, fleece is the most common. Regardless of which coat type the Cavapoo has, the dog looks like a fuzzy teddy bear.

The Cavapoo's coat may be curly, silky or wavy. Their long ears are probably one of the Cavapoo's most distinctive features.

Size

This pooch is the perfect size for most homes and apartments. They will weigh between 10-20 pounds and stand 9-14 inches tall. Those bred with Toy Poodles will be lighter and smaller whereas those bred with Miniature Poodles will be bigger.

The size of the Cavapoo depends on the size of the parents. Since either a Toy or Miniature Poodle may be used, their size can vary. Their weight ranges from 7 to 18 pounds and they usually stand between 9" to 14" tall at the shoulder.

Coat

Most Cavapoos have a soft, curly or wavy coat depending on which genes they inherit – Poodle or Cavalier King Charles Spaniel (which also means they could be hypoallergenic). While his coat can be maintained by regular bathing followed by brushing to prevent tangles, it's recommended that a visit to a professional groomer be scheduled every four to six weeks. The breed is also known to experience those reddish-brown tear stains, a malady that can be addressed by washing his face daily with careful attention paid to the area beneath his eyes.

Colors

You have a rainbow of colors to choose from with this breed. The most popular colors include: fawn, black and tan, ruby, white and black and cream. They a come in other variety of different colors also , including, gold, tricolor (black, white and tan) or Blenheim (brown and white).

Puppies

Predictably, the small Cavapoo produces an even smaller puppy, so care must be taken to ensure he is safeguarded from extremes such as heat, cold, and even well-meaning kids who can play rough. Because the breed is highly intelligent and eager to please, training can begin during the puppy stage and early socialization will be key to ensuring he is comfortable with strangers and other pets. This tiny dog will learn quickly though, so it's worth getting any heavy training out of the way early to ensure that you have a well behaved pup.

Height & Weight

Male: 10-14 inches 10-20 pounds

Female: 9-14 inches 10-15 pounds

Health Concerns

Cavapoos usually live long and happy lives with good care from responsible owners. Generally speaking, as they are the mixed breed between Poodle and Cavalier King Charles Spaniel, they could inherit some of the conditions from both species. However, they are usually more resilient than their parents, thanks to the "hybrid vigor" – improved function of all biological systems – gained in the mixing process.

However, they do, sometimes, have problems with their eyes, heart and knees. They are also prone to dental problems, problems with their ears and epilepsy. As every other dog species, they also need a daily exercise routine to stay fit and satisfied. However, due to their small stature, they don't need a lot of space to run around. A medium-sized yard or one daily walk around the block, along with some playtime inside, is enough to keep them in good shape.

Cavapoos are prone to diseases seen commonly in both Cavalier King Charles Spaniels as well as poodles. As their popularity in the US has grown, more and more cavapoo breeders have cropped up. Reputable breeders will screen their cavapoos, spaniels, and poodles for these illnesses and will not breed dogs that have a disease that has a genetic component. Health problems commonly seen in cavapoos can include:

- Congenital Heart Defects: The most common being mitral valve disease, where a valve in a dog's heart is malformed and, thus, doesn't fully occlude when closed
- Progressive Retinal Atrophy (PRA): An ocular disorder that can lead to blindness
- Luxating Patellas: An orthopedic issue where the groove that the kneecap rests in is shallow, allowing the kneecap to pop in and out of place
- Atopy: Also known as skin allergies in dogs
- Syringomyelia/Chiari-Like Malformation: This is a condition in which pockets of fluid build up in your dog's spinal cord
- Dental Disease: Infections and abscesses of your dog's teeth that can be painful

In contrast, dogs such as the Cavalier King Charles Spaniel are more likely to encounter health issues like:

- Mitral valve dysplasia
- Chiari-like malformation
- Diabetes mellitus

- Idiopathic epilepsy
- Urolithiasis (stones)

The general health conditions of Cavapoos:

- Eye Conditions

Cavapoos may suffer from progressive retinal atrophy, which is a degenerative eye disease leading to blindness. This condition is hereditary and is not yet fully understood. Some of the symptoms include reluctance to go downstairs or refusing to go outside when it is dark or dim.

There is still no treatment for this disorder, but if your dog develops it, the best you are able to do is to adapt its living space to allow easy movement and improve the quality of its life.

- Heart Problems

This breed may suffer from congenital heart problems, as well, such as the Mitral Valve disease. It is usually spotted at regular veterinarian check-ups, as the faulty valve makes murmurs that are easy to hear with a stethoscope.

- Slipping Kneecaps

Inherited malformations or injuries of the kneecaps may cause them to jump sideways out of their place. This is very painful and the dog is not able to use the affected leg. Treatment usually involves anti-inflammatory drugs, but sometimes, surgery is also required. However thanks to this mixes' hybrid vigor this mix tends to be healthier than most purebreds.

Others health problems includes:

- Hip dysplasia: This is a condition that affects the hip joint and reduces mobility.
- Mitral Valve Heart Disease: This disease is a genetic condition that can affect Cavalier King Charles Spaniels. It often results in the degeneration of the mitral valve.
- Epilepsy: This is a neurological condition that causes seizures and sadly is often seen in some Poodles.

So How Long Do Cavapoos Live For?

Despite having this massive list of health problems, rest assured that a healthy, well-cared for Cavapoo is going to have a long lifespan. As mentioned in the first paragraph they can live anywhere from 10 to 15 years!

Responsible Owners

Buy Cavapoo puppies only from responsible breeders that are careful about the inherited health problems and screen their dogs before breeding, using only the healthiest and best-looking dogs.

However, even the most careful breeders don't have the power to prevent every possible health problem, so it is your responsibility to provide your pet with the best possible healthcare and to watch out for the biggest problem in small dogs – obesity.

Responsible breeders will often have the parents undergo genetic screening to determine if the parents are healthy from certain diseases such as hip dysplasia or genetic eye problems. This is beneficial because the breeders are then able to offer the buyer some sort of guarantee in writing.

Cavapoo Care

Caring for the Cavapoo is fairly straight forward. This pup's small size makes them easy to feed and as a companion breed they do not need lots of exercise. The most tedious part of caring for this teddy bear pup is grooming their curly coat.

Unless you know how to trim a dog's coat, it is likely that you will need to spend a few bucks at the groomer's to keep their coat nice. Apart from that, this is a fuss free pooch.

Exercise

Although one of their parents is a working dog, the Cavapoo does not need a high amount of exercise. This pooch is often happy with short periods of play followed by resting.

Two or three short walks (15 minutes) each day is enough for this breed. This will leave them tired enough until the next walk or play session. Because the Cavalier King Charles Spaniel is a hunting breed it is likely your Poodle mix will be too. So off-leash walking is not recommended for this breed.

An activity that would work wonders for your Cavapoo would be hiking. Not only will your pooch be exposed to exciting scents and sights, but they will also get the chance to spend quality time with their favorite people.

- Total Daily Activity: 30 minutes.
- Activity Level: 2/5.
- Favorite Activity: Playing in garden.

How Much Exercise Do They Need?

Cavapoos may be mellow, gentle and affectionate dogs that are perfectly content laying with you on the couch, but don't let that fool you. They have a high-energy drive and love running around as much as possible. They should have at least 30 to 60 minutes of good exercise every day but will not complain at all if they get even more.

Don't feel compelled to limit the exercise to just daily walks or running around the yard. Cavapoos are intelligent dogs that love brain games and mental stimulation. Despite how much the dog will enjoy food-filled treats and games, keep them to a minimum to prevent overeating because this dog will not walk away from a delicious treat.

Cavapoos love daily exercise and literally thrive ongoing for daily walks or family playtime, which might include playing fetch, jumping or just romping with the children. Because they're such high-energy dogs, you might feel as though they never tire out. You can read more about exercise and get some fun ideas, here.

Interactive toys and puzzles are a great way to help provide the Cavapoo with the extra stimulation and satisfaction he may require after this daily exercise. He may not yet be 100% tired even if his owner is.

Grooming

One of the best things about owning a Cavapoo is their lovely and curly coat. However this is also one of the more challenging parts of caring for this lovable breed. Their coat is prone to matting if it is not cared for properly. Lots of first time keepers find it hard to learn how to groom the coat so they pay for a professional groomer.

If you do decide to get them groomed you will need to take them once or twice a month. If you would rather save money (and have the time to do so) it is recommended that you groom your dog yourself.

Using a slicker brush for brushing sessions will be the best for this breed's curly coat. It will also help to keep their coat clipped short in either a teddy bear or puppy cut. While buying the equipment upfront will be on the costly side, this one-time purchase can be a smart investment and save you lots of money in the long run.

Overall grooming their curly Doodle hair is the hardest part of caring for this breed. If you can successfully groom them then the rest of their care is easy.

Food And Nutrition

Giving your Cavapoo a good nutritious diet is probably one of the best things you can do for him. They're a small breed dog and should have dog food that's specially made for small breed dogs and for the appropriate age. As a rule of thumb, small dogs like Cavapoos should get about 40 calories for each pound of dog weight. A 15-pound Cavapoo should get about 600 calories per day.

Most dog foods will list the serving size and the number of calories per serving size to make it easier to feed your Cavapoo the correct amount. Cavapoos should get about 480 to 950 calories per day when they're puppies and about 300 to

600 when they're adult dogs. Their daily requirements vary a lot on their size, which is also determined by whether the parent is a toy or miniature Poodle.

When it comes to feeding, serving breakfast and dinner for the Cavapoo is not a tough task. As they are a small breed they do not need lots of food. Anywhere from 1-1.5 cups of good-quality kibble is enough very active pooches will need a touch more than this. However remember that it is very easy to overfeed this breed, so pay close attention to their weight.

If you implement treats into the training program, make sure you offer nutritious treats and treats that will not pose a choking risk. Your veterinarian may be able to offer suggestions on the brand and type of dog food and dog treats that are best for your Cavapoo.

Cavapoos are adorable little dogs that respond very positively to treats, so it's even more important to make sure they get nutritious snacks as much as possible. Cavapoos do have a predisposition to over-eating, so it's important that when they do eat, it's healthy food to prevent the dog from becoming overweight.

Cavapoos tend to thrive on a diet made for smaller to medium sized, high energy breeds. Although the weight range for the breed doesn't seem that large, it can actually vary by a large percent! A 9 lb cavapoo is much smaller than a 20 lb cavapoo, and as such, will require much less food per day. Depending on the size of your cavapoo (and their activity level throughout the day) they may require anywhere from 1/2 C to 1 C food per day. Although they have a high energy level, if they are overfed (either with their daily food consumption or just extra cookies each day because they are just so darn cute) they can become overweight. Your veterinarian can help give you insight into how to help get the extra weight off your cavapoo, if this is the case

Socializing & Training

The Cavapoo requires socialization at an early age to ensure it grows to be a well-balanced dog familiar with different types of people, animals, situations, and environments. The earlier the socialization begins, the better it is for the dog. Socialization should include taking the dog to the park where he will be around other dogs and other people.

Taking Cavapoo for walks in the neighborhood will also help him get accustomed to his surroundings. You might also want to take them places that have loud noises to get them used to the noise. Lack of socialization often results in the dog becoming afraid of new things and barking or shying away with fear.

Training the Cavapoo is just as important as socialization and should begin at an early age. Despite being friendly and easy-going dogs, many owners claim that Cavapoos are hard to housetrain. Housebreaking the Cavapoo is best done with crate training. They are also sensitive dogs that don't respond well to yelling or harsh punishments or reprimands. Training sessions work best when they're short and end with positive reinforcement or treats. However, the training must be consistent. Cavapoos also respond well to praise and petting.

How To Train A Cavoodle

The Cavapoo's intelligence makes them very trainable – this is a trait given to them by their Poodle parent. However as the Cavalier King Charles Spaniel has a sensitive nature, the best way to train this breed is through positive reinforcement.

Positive reinforcement has many benefits. Your job is to make sure each training session is a positive experience, they can learn lots of tricks. Just remember because of their sensitive nature you should not use any aggression as this will make them scared and also make training an unpleasant experience. Socializing this breed is fairly easy (especially if it is with other dogs).

The Cavapoo is not naturally aloof and will enjoy spending time with other breeds. Just make sure to keep these socialization sessions short, sweet and positive to show them that meeting a new child or hearing the vacuum cleaner is not a scary experience.

When it comes to mental stimulation there is no need to spend hours on end training. As this breed is less of a working dog and more of a companion breed they do not need as much mental stimulation as the Poodle. Training will likely provide enough mental stimulation but it would not hurt to consider competing it in an obedience-based sport (such as rally).

Rally is very similar to agility courses except instead of jumping hurdles your pup performs certain skills (such as sit and stay).

Is The Cavapoo A Good Family Dog?

The Cavapoo's personality makes them a great family dog. They have the high-energy drive needed to keep up with older children while also possessing the gentleness and protective nature towards the younger ones. They're the happiest when they're the center of attention from all family members.

Is The Cavapoo Good With Kids?

Cavapoos are not only good family dogs but also dogs that are very good with children. If there were a checklist to determine qualities that make the Cavapoo a good dog, every box would be checked. Cavapoos are gentle and loving while also being playful and active. They seem to know what personality they should exhibit based on the child.

Because of their small size, they are quite attractive to small young children that might try to pick them up. Although Cavapoos are very good with kids, young children should be monitored when they're with the dog and taught to treat this dog with the same respect they would treat a large dog.

Do Cavapoos Shed?

Since Cavapoos may come in one of three different coat types, their ability or tendency to shed will depend on the coat they possess. Fleece coats, which are the most common, are low-shedding and require regular clipping to keep them that way. Fleece coats have either a curl or loose wave to them and feel very soft to the touch.

Hair coats may shed more but also require less brushing and clipping. The hair coat has a wiry and rough feel to it. Wool coats have tight curls and require brushing daily or frequent haircuts or both. Because wool coats release the least amount of dander and shed very little, they are the best coat type for people with allergies.

Maintenance

The type of coat type the Cavapoo has plays a role in the amount of care and maintenance the dog requires. It also determines who often the dog's coat should be brushed or trimmed to prevent tangling and matting. They also need their nails trimmed regularly and their ears clean to prevent infections. Cavapoos do best when kept inside the house. Although they enjoy playing outside, they don't do well when left outside alone for longer periods. Because of their short muzzle, they are very sensitive to heat.

Buyer's Tips

You should keep a list of recognized breeders. This is a very popular breed and once a litter becomes available they will likely be reserved within a day or two. Keep a list of reputable breeders you trust and set a calendar date for when their puppies will become available so you can beat the crowd and reserve a puppy yourself.

Just like other Doodle breeds this breed needs to be professionally groomed to keep their coat healthy. Make sure to set money aside each month so you are prepared for any necessary spa days.

If you are not able to set aside a fund for the groomer then consider getting a set of basic grooming supplies. The money you save by doing it yourself will add up over time. Plus your pup will be happier knowing its trusted owner is the one cutting its hair.

The Cavapoo is a breed that is content with a small selection of toys however you should not skimp on mental stimulation.

Because this breed is a people-dog you can take them outside around other people to give them stimulation. Not only will you save money on fancy toys, but you will also create lasting memories and make someone's day by letting them say hi to your pooch.

One great thing about this breed's popularity is that these dogs are available to buy in almost every state. One pitfall however is that puppy mills tend to take advantage of this. Be wary of Cavapoos being sold for less than $900 dollars that seem available year-round.

Where to Adopt or Buy a Cavapoo

Cavapoos are a relatively popular designer breed. Finding one shouldn't be as much of an issue as finding other, rarer breeds. The challenge is finding a reputable breeder. The breed's popularity makes them a popular choice for puppy mill breeders. General rules of thumb to avoid purchasing from a puppy mill is to avoid purchasing from pet shops (unless you live in a city in which pet shops are legally required to sell only shelter pets) and avoid breeders that don't let you see the parents and where they are kept.

Despite being considered a designer breed, cavapoos are also surrendered at shelters and rescues just as other breeds

31

unfortunately are. So if you are looking to rescue or adopt, finding one in a local shelter or rescue group should not be that difficult either. Speak to your veterinarian and local animal shelters about where to find a cavapoo if you are wanting to add one to your home.

Things You Need To Know If You're A First-Time Cavoodle Owner.

- The Cavoodle is easily considered one of Australia's most popular designer breed. In fact, some people believe that these lovely dogs may have actually originated from Australia.

- These sweet pups can get a little naughty sometimes. In such a case, we highly recommend that owners be patient, yet firm with training as the Cavapoo is not the kind of dog who'd respond to fear.

- They are considered hypoallergenic dogs! But, if they inherit more Cavalier King Charles Spaniel, then it's possible that their coats may no longer be "allergy-friendly."

- These doggies sometimes inherit the shorter-muzzles from their Spaniel lineage. As a result, they're very heat sensitive and so should not be left out too long on a hot summer's day.

- They are notorious for their soft nature. Because of this trait, many Cavapoos end up making great therapy dogs.

- They can have severe separation anxiety! Unfortunately, since these dogs thrive on human companionship, leaving them home alone for too long will be difficult—they'll let your neighbors know that by barking or crying till you come back!

- They are light eaters! As they are small dogs, your designer pup will consume one-two cups of kibble each day. I think this is a pro about the breed as you save on food costs!

- If your Cavapoo takes on the more Poodle-like fur, then they will not shed. However, if your pup inherits that silky coat from the Charles Spaniel, then they may be low-shedders.

- As they are people-pups, your pooch will have the tendency to get a little jealous, should he see you devoting your attention to another pet! Make sure he's not watching you when you give cuddles to your kitty!

- Cavoodles have small mouths and short muzzles. So, ensure they eat kibble designed for small dogs.

Do Cavapoos Need To Be Groomed & Bathed?

Cavapoos do need to be groomed and bathed, but the frequency in which they'll need it has a lot to do with their coat type. Keep in mind also that because they are a mixed breed you may not know what type of coat they're going to have until they're older. Cavapoos with wavy or curly coats will need regular brushing to prevent the hair from getting tangles and knots.

Two areas that are important to pay attention to are the armpits and the ears. Hair seems to grow long in the armpits and should be brushed and/or trimmed. The ears should be cleaned and wiped with a damp rag. Make sure they're dried thoroughly to prevent ear or yeast infections from developing. Cavapoos are very susceptible to developing ear infections, so cleanliness and keeping them dry is very important. Many Cavapoo owners also have the dog's teeth cleaned.

There really isn't any certain haircut specific to Cavapoos. Most owners use a teddy bear clip, which keeps leg and body hair short and the face round. The ears are generally kept straight and long like the Cavalier King Charles Spaniel.

Cavapoos usually need to go to the groomers every 8 to 10 weeks but only need to be bathed every 2 to 3 months.

Like training and socialization, grooming should begin at a very young age. The earlier in life the Cavapoo gets introduced to basic grooming, the better behaved he'll be at the groomers.

Roles – What Is This Breed Best Suited For?

The Cavapoo is a breed that is well-suited for many purposes. While their gentle, loving and playful nature make them ideal family pets, their intelligence, high trainability, and loyalty make them great service dogs. In addition, their ability to get along great with kids of all ages make them good companion and therapy dogs.

Although their small size may make the idea of Cavapoos hunting almost unbelievable, some Cavapoos enjoy hunting, especially in the water. Although this may come from both sides of the family, let's not forget that Poodles used to be great water hunting dogs! There really are very few purposes that the Cavapoo dog cannot fulfill.

How Much Does A Cavapoo Cost?

Upon deciding to buy a Cavapoo, don't be surprised to find that the cost of a Cavapoo varies by many factors. These factors include;

- Breeder's reputation
- Breeder's location
- Puppy's lineage
- Size of litter
- Supply and demand
- Socialization and training
- Age of puppy

When we think in terms of crossbreed dogs, we generally think of dogs that are cheap because they're not purebred. While this was usually the case in the past, it's not often the same today, at least not with the Cavapoo dog. Cavapoos cannot be registered with the American Kennel Club because they're a mixed breed dog, but the parents may be purebred and registered with the AKC in their respective breed registry (Poodle or Cavalier King Charles Spaniel).

Cavapoos may be registered with the International Designer Canine Registry. This may also affect the cost of the

Cavapoo. The average price for a Cavapoo is around $1,100, and this is for a Cavapoo without breeding rights and one that's not show-quality. Cavapoos can cost anywhere from $1,000 to $10,000 or more. Cavapoos may also be registered through these agencies.

- American Hybrid Club
- Dog Registry of American, Inc.
- Designer Breed Registry
- Designer Dogs Kennel Club

Finding Reputable Breeders Or Adopting

Once you decide to buy a Cavapoo, the biggest decision will probably be whether to get it from a breeder or through adoption at a rescue. Buying from a breeder can prove very time-consuming because you're going to want to make sure you only deal with a reputable breeder. Unless you know the breeder personally, it can be difficult knowing if you're dealing with a reputable and honest breeder.

Your vet or local animal shelter may be able to offer recommendations or offer help in locating reputable Cavapoo breeders. The Internet is also a great resource for information as well as a place to find reviews or recommendations on breeders.

How do you know if the breeder is reputable and honest or just another scammer or puppy mill? If the breeder shows any of these signs, you're probably best staying away.

- The breeders won't let you come to see his kennel.
- The breeder can't show you the puppy's mother and father.
- The kennel is not clean and orderly.
- The breeder deals with more than one breed of dog.
- The price of the puppies is too good to be true.
- The breeder is not willing to give any kind of guarantee.
- The breeder insists on a deposit without providing a receipt.
- The breeder is hesitant or unwilling to answer all your questions.

Adopting a Cavapoo is another way to become an owner of one of these beautiful dogs. The downside is that you probably won't have your choice of a puppy because it will most likely be coming from a rescue or shelter group. AnimalLeague.org offers information on finding Cavapoos through shelter or rescue groups. You'll be expected to pay adoption fees, which cover the cost of medical care and sterilization, but you'll also be saving a dog from euthanasia. The price to adopt a Cavapoo can range from about $250 to $800.

Real Owner/Breeder Recommended Supplies

We've scoured the web to compile the most recommended supplies by actual Cavapoo owners and reputable breeders. We've taken it a step further and have personally researched each product to ensure it's worthy of our stamp of approval as well. cool If you don't see something you're looking for here, be sure to check our personal recommended products page.

- Crate
- Brush

Most owners and groomers recommend a slicker brush for a Cavapoo, which makes sense because slicker brushed work well on dogs mixed with the Poodle. This slicker recommended by professional groomers all over because of their quality and because each pin is rounded on the end. This is important to avoid discomfort when you're brushing them.

- Comb

Groomers will tell you that a good comb is just as important as a brush. They make brushing soo much easier, too. It is advised to use the comb first, to make sure all the tangles are out, and for sensitive areas like around the face.

They Deserve the Spa Treatment

Cavapoo sitting on a blue backgroundApart from general grooming and brushing, it's vital also to remember to groom your pet's nails, ears, and eyes. Starting with their paws, you'll need to make sure that their nails are kept short and well trimmed back.

Now, if you've got a very active pup who plays a lot outdoors, then this good as they have the potential to wear out their nails and so require less npoodlail trimming.

Secondly, watch out for eye staining problems! Poodles are quite prone to runny eyes which stains their fur reddish-brown. So, many Cavoodles also get these stained-eye problems. To prevent this from happening you should clean your pup's eyes with tear stain remover wipes often.

Lastly, these pups need to have their ears cleaned and checked on a regular basis. Dog's with big,

long, floppy ears are very often more prone to ear infections. In fact, Poodles have sensitive ears and are at risk of developing ear infections. Since your hybrid is going to be a relatively "fluffy" dog, make sure the fur around and in their ears are well trimmed.

What Kind Of Home Grooming Tools Do I Need?

The most important thing you need to know about their coats is that it is going to be very prone to matting, tangles, knots, and catching all that dirt they play around in! So, make sure you prepare yourself by purchasing a few grooming tools.

The first essential brush you'll need are those two-sided pins and bristle brush. These brushes are ideal for removing any tangles and dirt. Now, these brushes also straighten out their curly hair. So, when you brush your dog's coat with the bristle side, you can expect to see an increase in frizziness.

The second item you'll need is a wide-tooth metal comb. The purpose of these comes is to de-mat fur and loosen tangles.

41

Conclusion

These days, the adorable Cavapoo remains one of the most popular breeds on the planet, despite most of the time not being able to predict the size, color, or coating of your future pup. Regardless of this gambling scenario, their temperament and overall personality is the primary determinant of why the hybrid has become this well-known across the globe.

Having been proven as a loyal, kind, intelligent and charming dog, the Cavapoo is an excellent addition to any family looking to expand and bring in a tiny, yet lively element of fun through their front doors.

If you are searching for a down to earth companion then look no further than the Cavapoo. These companion dogs will steal your heart with their gentle personalities and intelligence. They are very trainable and make the perfect companion if you work from home or are a homebody. If you can afford to professionally groom them then this is the best option.

Any other form of care besides grooming comes easy. While the world is always busy and bustling, the laid-back and gentle Cavapoo will be by your side and eager to make your day. These dogs are simply easy to adore and fall in love with.

Printed in Great Britain
by Amazon